TRIUMPH
BONNEVILLE T120

1959 - 1974

Roy Bacon

NITON PUBLISHING

First published in the United Kingdom by:
Niton Publishing
PO Box 3 . Ventnor . Isle of Wight PO38 2AS

Acknowledgements
The author would like to thank those who
helped this book by supplying the photographs. Most came from the EMAP archives
or *Motor Cycle News* by courtesy of the
Editor, Malcolm Gough. Others came from
the Mick Woollett archive, one from Ivor
Davies and some from the author's files.

© Copyright Roy Bacon 1989

Filmset and printed by Crossprint
Newport . Isle of Wight

ISBN 0 9514204 4 5
A CIP catalogue record for this book is
available from the British Library

Front Cover: Taken from a 1965 Triumph brochure and shows the big twin in a
stylish scene from those times.

Back Cover: A pre-unit T120 taken from the 1961 brochure.

Bernal Osborne outside the Meriden works on a 1963 Bonneville, the first year for unit construction for the 650 model.

Contents

Introduction

The Bonneville first appeared in Triumph's 1959 range, almost as an afterthought; beginning its highly successful life as a twin-carburettor Tiger 110. It soon became a model in its own right and, through the 1960s, was one of THE machines to own, offering both style and performance.

In 1963 the engine and gearbox were changed to unit construction, without altering its concept one iota, but the Bonneville was to stumble a little in 1971 when given a new frame and inordinately high seat. In time, this problem was overcome and the Bonneville continued into the convulsions of the 1970s and the Meriden sit-in. By then, the original T120 had been joined by the larger T140 and it was the latter that emerged from the cauldron of the upheaval, to run on for another decade.

That, as they say, is another story for this one only concerns the original T120 Bonneville - a great motorcycle.

The great Henry Cooper and his brother on a pre-unit T120 at a show.

The Bonneville arrives

The Triumph twin began its life late in 1937 as the 499 cc Speed Twin, was quickly joined by the Tiger 100 Sports version and, post-war, its engine size was increased to create the 649 cc Thunderbird for 1950. For a while, this met the cry for more capacity and power but, by 1954, the Tiger 110 had to be created from it to meet the demand.

A light-alloy cylinder head went on to the Tiger 110 for 1956 and the following year saw the first optional head with splayed inlet ports. This appeared on the Tiger 100, which previously had had a twin-carburettor option on parallel ports, and for 1958 a splayed-head option was offered for the Tiger 110.

Included in the list of high-performance parts that became available at the same time were a pair of Amal racing GP carburettors, remote float chamber, hotter camshafts and a host of pure racing details for both engine and cycle. Many were listed

First of the Bonneville line was the 1959 model which was alone in having the Triumph nacelle and a dynamo.

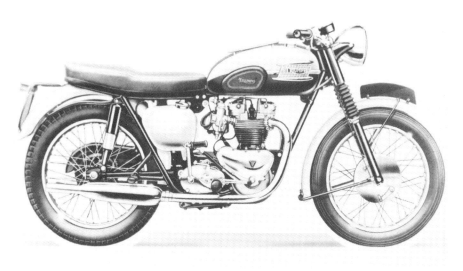

Bonneville T120 in its 1960 form with new frame and duplex downtubes which was quickly revised after some breakages.

solely that they could be used in production racing and not all were too easy to buy from your friendly Triumph dealer.

This added up to an untidy situation, so for 1959 the firm - meaning Edward Turner who ran it in an autocratic manner and made instant decisions - introduced the Tiger 120 as the Bonneville. The specification was basically that of the twin-carburettor T110 and the name an acknowledgement of the performance of the streamlined Triumph ridden by Johnny Allen at Bonneville salt flats in September 1956. The FIM, international governing body of motorcycle sport, refused to ratify the speed as a world record, on a technicality, but everyone else knew that the machine had run at 214 mph.

The speed run and the row that ensued between Triumph and the FIM brought tremendous publicity to the firm, enhancing the demand for the more powerful version of the Tiger 110. Hence the rapid appearance of the splayed-port head, twin carburettors and, in time, the Bonneville.

The Tiger 120 could thus trace its engine ancestry straight back to the first Speed Twin of 1937 for it had the same lines and engine build. Its 649 cc capacity came from engine dimensions of 71 x 82 mm and it was a 360 degree parallel twin with equal firing intervals; the norm for the British industry.

Construction of the engine was based on a vertically-split crankcase cast in aluminium and separate from the gearbox. The split was on the

Drive side of the 1961 Bonneville, beloved transport of the cafe racer set.

engine centre-line and the case halves had an identical ball-race main bearing in each side plus two bronze bushes, one for each camshaft.

The crankshaft itself was forged in one-piece, the flywheel being pressed on to its centre and held in place by three radial bolts. An oil seal ran on the crankshaft just out-

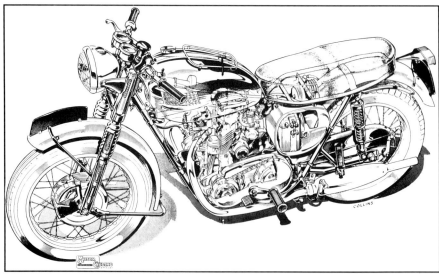

Line drawing of the 1961 T120 showing its general layout and some details of construction.

board of the left drive-side main but on the right there was only the timing pinion. This drove an idler that meshed with camshaft gears, the shafts themselves running across the crankcase, high up and to front and rear of the crankshaft. The left-hand end of the rear, inlet camshaft drove a timed disc-valve breather.

A cast-iron block was held down on the crankcase mouth by eight studs and nuts. It had two tappet

of the valve wells in the cylinder head, with seals top and bottom to keep the oil in. The seals were to be the subject of a good few changes during the life of the T120.

The pistons that ran in the block each had three rings, including the scrapers, and gave a compression ratio of 8.5:1. They were fixed to light-alloy, forged connecting rods by gudgeon pins retained by circlips. The rods had bushed small-

Final year for the pre-unit Bonneville was 1962 with few changes from the previous two.

blocks pressed into it on the centre line, to front and rear, for exhaust and inlet respectively. Each block carried two tappets which had radiused feet that bore on the cam to transmit its form to the pushrods and the overhead valves. The pushrods were concealed within plated steel tubes, which ran from the tappet blocks to the underside

ends and plain big-ends with renewable shells. Each rod cap was assembled with two ground bolts and nuts, which were tightened to a bolt-stretch figure.

The one-piece cylinder head was an aluminium casting held down on the block and head gasket by eight evenly-spaced bolts. It had splayed inlet ports that were threaded for

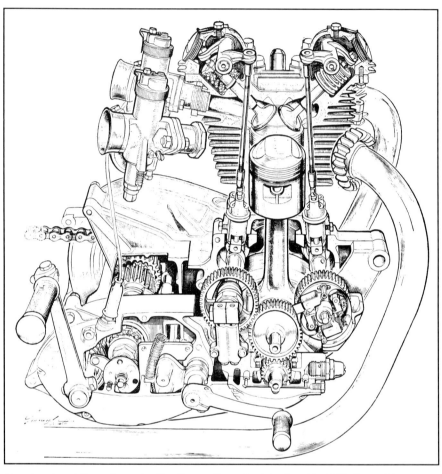

Line drawing of the unit construction Bonneville engine introduced in 1963 along with a revised frame.

the inlet tracts which screwed into place and each was then locked by a large nut. Twin Amal Monobloc carburettors of 1-1/16 in. bore were used and these were 'chopped' so that they had no float chamber section. This duty was carried out by a round Amal Grand Prix chamber clamped to the seat tube with a rubber strip round it to reduce the effects of vibration. Thus, the chamber sat neatly between the two carburettor bellmouths and was supplied by fuel lines from twin petrol taps with a T-pipe feed to the mixing chambers.

The exhaust ports were also threaded, a plain tubular adaptor being screwed in for the exhaust pipe to clamp to. This was done with a finned collar and both pipes and the tubular silencers were common with the T110.

There were wells in the cylinder head for each pair of valves, which slid in guides that were pressed in to a shoulder. The guides also acted as a location for the seating for the duplex coil springs which were retained by a collar and split collets.

A rocker box went over each valve well and had a single spindle, drilled for lubrication, for its pair of rockers. Spring and hardened washers were included in each assembly to reduce noise and wear, while each rocker had an adjuster screw and locknut at its outer end for setting the valve gap. Access for this was via a screwed cap in each corner of each rocker box, a distinctive Triumph feature - as was their habit of becoming unscrewed and vanishing into the ditch.

The lubrication system was dry-sump with an external oil tank and a twin-plunger pump driven by an off-centre pin. This was part of the nut that secured the inlet camshaft gear to its shaft and the pump itself was bolted to the timing chest below this. It delivered its output to a pressure release valve, set in the timing cover, which incorporated an indicator button to comfort the owner.

From the release valve the oil went to a cavity in the timing cover.

Primary chaincase, battery cover and twin Amal Monoblocs of the 1961 T120 with magneto ignition but alternator for the current.

In this was a bush, in which the extreme right-hand end of the crankshaft ran, and the oil was fed into the centre of the mainshaft. It passed via drillings to the two big-ends and then drained down to the sump. This was a plate located at the base of the crankcase and the assembly included a gauze filter. A pipe was it drained back down the pushrod covers, over the cams and into the sump.

Ignition was by a Lucas K2F magneto with manual advance as standard but there were options of auto-advance, a competition version of either and a racing K2FR. Whichever was used, it was fitted on three

The revamped Bonneville on show with a crowd of admirers dreaming of the open road and fast bends.

fixed to the inside of the right-hand crankcase half and connected the area beneath the sump filter with a drilling which communicated with the oil scavenge pump.

Thus the oil was collected and returned to the tank but any fault in the internal pipe would prevent this and cause a build up of oil in the crankcase. A feed for the rocker spindles was taken from the return line near the tank, a small-bore pipe carrying the oil up to the top of the engine. Once the oil had done its job

studs in the rear of the timing chest behind the crankcase. It was gear driven, its pinion being meshed with that of the inlet camshaft.

Current for the 6 volt electrical system was generated by a Lucas E3L dynamo which was clamped to the front of the engine by a strap. Like the magneto, it was gear driven, but from the exhaust camshaft and the dynamo pinion was small enough to pass through the drive hole in the back of the timing chest. For competition work the dynamo could be

Bernal Osborne on the 1963 Bonneville at the Meriden works.

removed and replaced by a rev-counter drive gearbox but this was not practical where full electrics had to be retained.

A single cover enclosed all the timing gears plus the oil pump and was attached by a series of small screws. It included the pressure release valve and crankshaft-end bush, while the outside face carried

The engine sprocket was splined directly to the crankshaft and drove back to the clutch with a single-strand primary chain. A shock-absorber was built into the hub of the multi-plate clutch which had bonded inserts for its five driving plates. These were clamped to the plain plates by four extra strong coil springs, which were a standard fit-

The 1964 Bonneville in the form which was not to alter much for some years and was THE machine to own.

a small triangular plate with the T120 model number. An alternative cover with a rev-counter drive was listed for those who desired it and the gearbox was built into it taking its drive from the exhaust camshaft. A suitable bracket was listed to carry both the rev-counter head and the speedometer.

ment for the T120 and an option for the other twins.

The primary transmission was enclosed by a nicely styled and polished chaincase, cast in two parts in aluminium. A row of small screws held the halves together and a screw cap in the shoulder of the outer enabled oil to be poured in and the

Engine unit of a 1964 T120 which retained much from the past in new alloy castings.

chain tension to be checked. At the rear of the chaincase was a spring-loaded needle-valve screw which allowed a controlled oil feed from the case to lubricate the rear chain.

The clutch was fitted to the main-shaft of the four-speed footchange gearbox which was a separate unit and thus movable to allow the primary chain tension to be set. The gearbox was the standard assembly used by the other road models ex-

Timing side of the 1965 Bonneville with its sleek lines so admired by riders of the day - and now.

For riders who sought something that stood out Dave Degens offered his Dresda version in café racer style.

cept that it alone dispensed with the Slickshift clutch mechanism. This linked the gear pedal movement so that it also raised the clutch, but was not too popular with owners and never used on the T120. For that model the simple lever mechanism with a hardened screw adjuster to bear on the clutch pushrod was used.

The gearbox was typically British, having a sleeve gear concentric with the mainshaft and carrying a final drive sprocket inboard of the clutch. The layshaft had the speedometer drive gear pinned to one end and ran in flanged bushes. The moving gears were controlled by selector forks which slid on a common spindle under the control of a circular camplate. This was rotated

by a positive stop mechanism that terminated in a pedal with typical Triumph up-for-up gearchange pattern.

An alternative pedal, giving heel-and-toe movement, was available as was a folding kickstart pedal. The latter operated a quadrant, returned by a clock spring, which meshed with a ratchet gear on the right-hand end of the mainshaft. Within the gearbox there were standard ratios but options of wide or close ratios were available for those who sought them.

The engine and gearbox were supported by plates fore and aft, the latter running back and up over the gearbox. All were fitted into a frame that was built up in the traditional way from tubes brazed into forged lugs and with a bolted on subframe. The main part comprised the headstock with top, seat and downtubes, the top one being braced by another beneath it. The subframe completed the main loop and had duplex tubes that ran from the bottom of the downtube, picked up with the seat tube, ran back and up to the tops of the rear units and then forward to the junction of the top and seat tubes. Cross-members braced it and both prop and centre stands were included in the assembly.

The rear fork was made in the same way as the frame and had a bush pressed into the forward end of each leg tube. It pivoted on a pin pressed into a massive lug that was brazed to the seat tube while a spacing washer controlled the side play, with shims being available to take up wear. Unfortunately, these could only be fitted by removing the pin, which often proved to be beyond the facilities of the home mechanic.

Lubrication of the pin was best done with a high-pressure grease gun and without it, wear and sometimes seizure could occur. An oversize pin was available to cope with wear in the frame lug, but the whole system was difficult to service at home and none too effective in use.

The Thruxton Bonneville produced for a short time in 1965 with fairing, humped seat, rearsets and other necessities for production racing.

Aside from wear, the loading of the whole fork and wheel had to be taken by the seat tube alone which was hardly in the best position to resist twisting forces.

Girling rear units with three load positions and hydraulic damping controlled the fork and were fitted as standard with 100lb rate springs. Options from 90 to 150 lb were available as were units from other firms. Full shrouds kept the springs out of sight and offered protection to the damper struts and seals.

At the front went the standard forks, complete with the famous Triumph nacelle, although 1959 was to be the only year it appeared on the Bonneville. Each fork leg had an internal spring so the forks were slim even though the nacelle was extended down to form a shroud for each leg. The fork leg ends were split for the wheel spindle and the forks were hydraulically damped.

A steering damper was provided and, so owners of other marques claimed, was essential. The damper itself went under the lower crown with a control knob above the top crown and the nacelle top. This part carried the speedometer with the ammeter, light switch and cut-out knob behind it. The first ran up to 120 mph or 180 kph depending on the country it went to and an optional 240 kph head was available. Chrome-plated side flashes con-

Little alteration for a 1965 T120 as it delivered what customers wanted.

Timing side of the unit construction Bonneville engine with points in the timing cover but still breathing from twin Monoblocs.

cealed the junction of the top and lower nacelle sections and these all combined to hold the headlamp unit. Beneath it went a plated horn grille with the Lucas horn behind it.

The front wheel had a full-width composite hub built up from steel pressings and a cast-iron drum brazed and riveted together. A pressed, chrome-plated nave plate enclosed the left-hand side and an 8 in. single-leading-shoe brake went on the right. The hub was laced to a steel rim of WM2 section with straight spokes and the assembly fitted with a 3.25 x 19 in. ribbed tyre.

At the rear went a wheel with offset brake drum combined with the rear wheel sprocket. The hub itself had smaller flanges and bent spokes which were laced to the same rim size as the front but was fitted with a 3.50 x 19 in. studded tyre. A

quickly detachable wheel was available as an option and differed from the standard one in the connection between hub and brake drum. The standard version was bolted but the quickly detachable had drive splines between the two parts with a sealing ring between them to keep the weather at bay. Each rear wheel had a 7 in. single-leading-shoe brake, the backplate being held by a torque stay fixed to the left-hand rear fork leg.

Despite the sporting nature of the Bonneville it was fitted with the same mudguards and number plates as the other road models, only the off-road TR6 having something more suitable. Thus the T120 had well valanced mudguards, the front one being held by a fork bridge and a rear stay that doubled as a front stand. The number plate had the

New tank badges for a 1966 Bonneville which continued the line and style with the rev-counter drive from the exhaust camshaft end.

bright surround first seen back in 1939 and this was another well-known Triumph trade mark. At the rear, the mudguard was supported by a lifting handle which ran along on both sides. A rubber mudflap was listed as an extra for the rear mudguard.

The oil tank was tucked into the corner of the subframe on the right and matched by a combined tool-box and battery carrier on the left. The two were joined at the front and also normally provided a home for the air filter but this was not speci-fied for the T120.

A dualseat was provided for the rider and passenger, the machine starting life with the standard road model type. During the year the narrower and more sporting type, used by the TR6, was adopted but not for all export models to the USA, some of which had a safety strap fitted.

The standard petrol tank had a 4 gallon capacity and was styled as others of that period. Thus it had grille badges ahead of kneegrips with a styling band running between the two and ahead of the badge. There was also a plated strip over the top central seam and the popular parcel grid was fitted to the tank as stan-dard. The filler cap was of the quar-ter-turn type and the same features and fittings were used on the 3 gallon export tank.

Standard or high-rise American handlebars were listed and both carried the combined horn button and dipswitch on the back of the clutch lever block. There was no air lever for the T120 but it did have a magneto advance on the bars along with the usual front brake lever and twistgrip.

The finish was mainly black with just the petrol tank and mudguards coloured. At first, the tank top and mudguards were in pearl grey with the lower tank and mudguard stripes in tangerine. Later, this was altered to royal blue for the lower tank and stripes, while the pearl grey was extended to include the oil tank and toolbox.

It added up to an exciting motorcycle in both looks and performance, one that was immediately in demand and at the start of a long, successful run. It was fast, it could be made faster, and it slotted straight into the sports requirements of the times.

Pre-unit development

The Bonneville underwent some significant changes for 1960, for it was given a new frame, lost its nacelle and adopted alternator electrics. The frame was still in two parts but the front section was now a complete loop with duplex downtubes that ran under the engine to the seat tube. This was simply a continuation of the top tube and early examples lacked bracing under this, which caused some to break. A lower tank rail was soon added to cure this fault.

The subframe was still bolted in place and the rear fork kept its awkward servicing with the pressed-in pivot pin. Control remained by Girling units and overall there seemed to be little real alteration, except for the duplex tubes at the front.

The 1966 T120 from the timing side and still fitted with dualseat with smooth top.

Drive side of the standard 1966 Bonneville with the electric switches under the seat.

Because the nacelle had been removed the forks were changed to the TR6 pattern with gaiters to protect the stanchions. In other respects the forks were as before except that a full, chrome-plated headlight shell was now used and held by the ears of the short upper fork shrouds. It carried the amme-ter and had a plug to connect to the quickly-detachable socket in the wiring harness. This was known to work loose and the result could be instant darkness - not too popular with riders.

Further electrical changes were to a magneto with auto-advance and an alternator in place of the dynamo,

The off-road T120TT built for the USA with open exhaust pipes and no lights, energy transfer ignition and 11:1 compression ratio.

The standard road Bonneville was built in this form for the USA and listed as the T120R in 1966.

whose removal brought a change to the crankcase and timing cover. The addition of the alternator, a Lucas RM13/15, meant a new chaincase as the stator was fitted in this with the rotor on the left-hand crankshaft end. Finally, the light switch had to be given a new home and was moved to a bracket under the seat nose on the right, while the cut-out button was moved from the nacelle to the handlebars.

Other alterations affected the mudguards which became the sports blade type as fitted to the TR6. The rear stay of the front one continued as a front stand but a front stay appeared and ran to a point halfway down the fork legs. At the top of the forks a bracket was provided for the speedometer and for this, there was a choice of a 125

mph or 240 kph head.

The float chamber was no longer the racing type or clamped to the seat tube but was changed to an adaption of the type 6 Amal chamber. This was suspended from a rubber mounting so it could be easily adjusted for height. It continued to have a single outlet to a T-pipe, which was linked to the mixing chamber banjos.

The rear wheel sprocket was reduced in size and the engine sprocket adjusted to return the gearing to near its previous figure. A seal was added to the oil indicator to prevent leakage and this completed the changes. The finish continued as it had been for the latter part of 1959 except that the headlamp shell was chrome-plated.

More alterations appeared for

1961 when the remote float chamber was dispensed with and twin standard Monoblocs used instead. They were fed from a smaller 3 gallon tank and supplied mixture to a cylinder head that had a vertical runner added to the outside of each exhaust port.

The gearbox changed to needle races for the layshaft and a folding kickstart lever as standard while the gearing was lowered by one tooth on the engine sprocket. Both wheels had floating brake shoes, which automatically centred in the drum, and the rear changed to a WM3 rim and a 4.00 x 18 in. tyre. The home market speedometer became a 140 mph type.

The Bonneville had previously been listed as the T120 or T120R, the latter being the export road version, often with raised bars and a small tank. There was also a T120C or competition model, which went further, mainly for the American West Coast and off-road use. For this, there were the usual bars and tank plus waist-level exhaust systems along each side, heat shields on the pipes to protect the rider, an undershield and trail tyres.

The finish was amended for 1961 to a format that the Bonneville was to keep for most of the decade. It was mainly black with chrome-plated wheel rims and headlamp shell. The petrol tank and mudguards were usually two-tone and, for 1961, the tank top and mudguard strips were in sky blue while the lower tank and mudguards were in silver. For that year only, the silver was also applied to the oil tank and battery box.

1962 was the final year for the pre-unit Bonneville and there were few changes introduced for it. The crankshaft was revised with a new balance factor while the alternator

A 1966 Bonneville won by a MCN reader in one of their competitions and no doubt very pleased about it.

Bob Currie out road testing a Bonneville in 1966 and enjoying a fast ride on a fine machine.

was uprated to an RM19. The purchaser was given the option of a 3 or 4 gallon petrol tank and both oil tank and battery box were revised. These last two items changed to a black finish but otherwise the home market finish was as 1961. For export, there was an alternative of Flame in place of the blue and, in this case, the oil tank and battery box remained in silver.

This brought the pre-unit model to the end of its days for it was to follow the rest of the range into unit construction. Some owners and riders thought this a retrograde step, for some found the effects of vibration more noticeable than in the past. On the other hand, it was nice not to have to move the gearbox to set the primary chain tension and, in the process, disturb the final drive.

Unit construction

The move to unit construction for the 649 cc engines was predictable as the smaller twins had begun to go that way as early as 1957. The larger ones combined the lessons used in that exercise with a good deal of the mechanics of the past, plus a degree of modernisation.

There were changes on the cycle side too, with a new frame and smaller wheels, but the Triumph twin line remained so there was no question as to the marque. With a carburettor poking out of each side there was also no possibility of mistaking the model for its single Monobloc cousin, the TR6. The latter had ceased to be built in its off-road form in 1960 to become, from then on, a single-carburettor T120. Many riders found it nearly as fast as the T120 and easier to keep in tune, but the Bonneville had the charisma so stayed at the top of Triumph's tree.

The new engine owed a good deal to the old one and, at first sight, used the same internals as the pre-unit engine. This was not quite so as, while a number of details were common, more were amended in one way or another. Thus, the crank-

The 1966 road test Bonneville at rest for the report photographs in front of the usual white sheet.

The Bonneville ridden by Steve Jolly and Malcolm Uphill at the Barcelona 24 hours race in 1969.

shaft kept its flywheel, held by three radial bolts, and plain big-ends while continuing to turn in the same main bearings of old. However, the extreme right-hand end of the crankshaft no longer ran in a bush in the timing cover but in a lip oil seal. This removed a wear point and improved the oil supply to the big-ends.

The timing gear stayed as it was and the left-hand end of the inlet camshaft continued to drive the breather disc, but the drive pinions were made wider. The exhaust camshaft had a drive taken from each end, that on the left being used for the rev-counter and that on the right for a contact breaker cam. This replaced the magneto, which was no longer specified, so the engine had coil ignition with a plate carrying two sets of points, set in the timing cover. The drive to the ignition cam included an auto-advance but both points sets were fixed to a single plate. With no adjustment between them this was to lead to many engines suffering because the timing was only exactly right on one cylinder.

Alloy connecting rods and three-ring pistons, giving an 8.5:1 compression ratio, continued in use along with the RM19 alternator on the left-hand end of the crankshaft. The oil pump was the faithful twin-plunger unit used by Triumph for so long and the release valve and indicator remained in the timing cover.

Engine unit of the 1967 T120 which was still much as before with those unmistakable Triumph lines.

For 1967 the Bonneville was fitted with a new dualseat with pleated top and a small rear hump.

The top half was amended slightly, the original eight head bolts being moved out from the bores a little and joined by a ninth. This went between the bores but in other respects the cast-iron block was really as before. Thus, there were the familiar tappet guide blocks fore and aft, surmounted by the chrome-plated pushrod tubes.

The cylinder head had its familiar Triumph form but the holding-

The Rickman Metisse road model with Bonneville engine in lovely duplex frame finished with nickel plating.

down bolt holes were moved to match the block. It still had both inlet tracts and exhaust stubs screwed into the ports and the same two Monobloc carburettors hung on the tracts. Construction of the rocker boxes was unchanged but each box was new with cooling fins along the front and sides. The valve caps were also altered and lost their spanner hexagons of old. Instead,

whole of the gearbox shell was part of the right-hand case. This case included the timing chest as of old, while the gearbox was a separate chamber, open to the right with a cover face further inboard than that of the timing chest.

The left-hand case included the inner wall of the primary chaincase which thus ran back alongside the gearbox sprocket. Access to this

The twin leading shoe front brake introduced on the Bonneville for 1968 and the only year the cable and levers were as this.

they had cross slots, so could be tightened with a coin or a steel bar. In addition, each had a serrated edge into which a locking spring, bolted to the rocker box, located. In theory, no more caps would vanish into the hedge.

The major new items were the crankcase halves which were now much larger and more extensive. The engine split remained on its centre-line but the join was then stepped over to the left so that the

was via a circular plate, complete with oil seal, which was held in place by six screws. The area above the sprocket was enclosed by the crankcase casting running back over it, while a frame mounting lug was cast above the top rear corner of the chaincase. The right-hand casting had a matching lug running up, back and left from the gearbox roof, while further lugs held the assembly in the frame.

With the gearbox fixed relative to

Standard 1968 Bonneville with access cover in the primary chaincase to allow the ignition timing to be checked with a strobe light.

the engine, the primary drive had to be amended, becoming a duplex chain tensioned with a slipper under the bottom run. This was set with a screw adjuster via an access plug in the lower rear end of the inner chaincase. The chain drove a six-plate clutch with bonded friction pads and three springs to clamp it. A shock absorber continued in the clutch centre and the assembly was much as before.

An outer chaincase enclosed the entire primary drive, was held by a

A 1968 T120 out on road test and going well as always, with Bob Currie again enjoying himself.

Show Bonneville with all the extras added for production racing in 1968.

series of small screws and had a single cap on the clutch centre to give access to the adjustment screw in the pressure plate. The filler cap was moved to the top of the inner chaincase and also gave access for checking the chain tension. Unfortunately, if adjustment was needed, removal of the tensioner plug also let all the oil out as it doubled as the drain; which was none too convenient. An oil feed for the rear chain was still taken from the primary chaincase but the flow was controlled by a jet so it was no longer adjustable. A blanking screw was available to block this feed line if required.

The clutch mechanism was changed to a design using three balls that ran up ramps, all fully enclosed within the gearbox covers. The gearbox itself remained as it was with many parts being carried over

from the pre-unit assembly. The change mechanism and positive stop details were the same other than for the minor amendments to suit the new castings and improvements such as an O-ring seal appearing on the gear-pedal shaft.

There were new gearbox covers to suit the revised crankcase but they continued to do the same jobs. The outer was altered to suit the new clutch mechanism and the shapes of both were blended into the new castings. The kickstart pedal remained of the folding type and was returned by the familiar clock spring but only the standard gear pedal was listed.

The complete engine unit presented a new line to the world from either side. On the left the chaincase now had a styling line so it lost the bulbous look that had come in with the alternator. For the right side the timing cover was now smaller and carried the points cover, while the separation of the gearbox was no longer so definite. It was also a far more rigid structure, which was to give the main bearings a harder time, for the case no longer flexed with the crankshaft and this loaded up the mains.

A new frame was introduced for the unit-construction engine but was still made in two sections. The front returned to its single downtube but remained a complete loop with duplex rails under the engine along with the single top and seat tubes. The subframe continued to be bolted in place and comprised a dualseat loop with a bracing tube on each side. These ran from the rear unit mounting to the ends of the under-engine rails.

The pivoted rear fork and its fixing to the frame were completely new and much improved. The fork was still fitted to a lug brazed to the single seat tube but now this lug spanned the fork cross-tube to carry the main pivot bolt with the fork between its two ears. The pivot bushes were pressed into the ends of the cross-tube and moved on inner sleeves assembled on the bolt. Hydraulically-damped, three-position, Girling spring units continued to control the rear end and were

A 1969 Bonneville out on test and fitted with the twin windtone horns introduced that year.

35

fitted with 145 lb rate springs.

The front forks continued as they were with gaiters to protect the stanchions and shroud lugs to carry the headlamp shell.There was still a steering damper and the wheel hubs were the same but spoked into 18 in. rims. The tyre sections reverted to 3.25in. for the front and 3.50 in. for the rear.

The remainder of the cycle parts were little altered from the pre-unit

a separate carrier and tray. A cover panel went on the left to match the oil tank and this carried the lighting and ignition switches, the latter with key, below the seat nose.

The finish for the first year of unit construction was Alaskan white for the tank and mudguards, the latter with a black stripe. The rest of the painted parts were in black and the headlamp shell and wheel rims chrome-plated. The modified T120R

Stock 1969 Bonneville with revised twin leading shoe front brake and no covers for the rear units.

model except where needed to suit the new frame. Thus, there were sports mudguards, centre and prop stands, a dualseat and the familiar Triumph tank with its grille badges and parcel grid. The area under the dualseat changed a little, although the oil tank remained on the right. It was no longer balanced by a combined battery and tool box, as these had been moved under the seat with

and T120C versions for the USA were also built and continued with their raised bars and variations of tank, wheels and exhaust systems. All models could have further high performance parts fitted but some of these tended only to be available to front runners in production racing. At times, this was to cause some dissension among owners, especially in racing paddocks.

The exhaust balance pipe was introduced for 1969 and the rocker box cap lock can also be seen.

There were new front forks for 1964 with external springs and revised damping. The steering damper remained but the handlebar clamps were no longer part of the top yoke, becoming eyebolts that were attached to it. For more power, the carburettors were changed to 1-1/8 in. type 389 Monoblocs and a balance pipe was added between the inlet tracts. Any increase in performance was now recorded by magnetic instruments which replaced the older chronometric type.

In 1964 the Bonneville's finish was changed to gold for the upper part of the petrol tank and the mudguard stripes but the lower tank and mudguards remained in Alaskan white. The rest of the painted parts were in black and the headlamp shell chrome-plated, with the whole a two-tone colour style which continued for several years with colour changes only. Thus, for 1965, it became Pacific blue for the tank top and guard stripes with silver for the tank lower and mudguards.

Little else altered for that year but the range was increased with the Thruxton Bonneville which was built purely for production racing. To this end it was fitted with all the high-performance options and came complete with rearsets and a fairing but it was only listed for some six months before being dropped. In general, racers preferred to build up their machines from the option range rather than have Triumph do this for them, while the firm had always tended to keep official racing at arm's length.

There were more changes for 1966

The T120R introduced for 1971 with new frame, forks and hubs but an engine much as the first with unit construction.

The final year of the first run of unit models was 1970 and this is the T120 for then .

when the colours became grenadier red and Alaskan white. For the range in general the electrical system was uprated to 12 volts with zener diode control of the generating system which was a great improvement. There were new tank badges of eyebrow style and distinctive handlebar grips in white, but the latter only lasted for the one season. Both wheels changed, a new rear brake drum, with a bolt-on sprocket for easy replacement, and rear-wheel drive for the speedometer being introduced at the back. The front hub remained a full-width type but with a flange on the drum side to stiffen it and this meant a return to bent spokes on that side although the other kept the straight ones. For the rear chain there was a metered oil feed from the oil tank with the control screw in the filler neck of the tank.

The official parts list now included the T120R, which had existed from pre-unit days, but not the T120C. It also showed the T120TT which had been a version of the T120C from 1964 with higher compression, well-tuned engine, larger carburettors, energy-transfer ignition, open exhausts and no lights. The result was a very fast off-road machine, demanding great skill and considerable muscle to exploit all its power.

The competition or C version of the T120 was only available in TT form for 1966, when the exhaust pipes were tucked in under the engine unit. In other respects it was as before with the tuned engine and stock cycle parts but included the 1966 changes where they applied. The T120TT did have different fork internals from stock, with a revised damper assembly, while it was fitted with sidecar-rate springs rather

A revamped Bonneville standing next to the smaller unit construction Trophy twin in 1971.

than solo ones.

Alterations for 1967 saw the compression ratio rise to 9:1 and only one switch, for the ignition, in the left side panel. The light switch was moved to the headlamp shell to be with the ammeter and they were joined by a pair of warning lights in red and green. The front wheel went back to a 19 in. rim but kept its 3.25 in. section tyre while the rear stayed as it was. The finish became purple, listed by Triumph as Aubergine, and Alaskan white but the USA models had purple top and gold lower for the petrol tanks plus stainless-steel mudguards.

More improvements were brought in for 1968, one being a change to Amal 930 Concentric carburettors which were fitted with drum air cleaners as standard, although the bellmouths remained an option. For the electrics there was a finned heat sink for the zener diode and achieving correct ignition timing was made much easier. This was done by making each set of points separate and giving each its own adjustable back plate, plus markings on the rotor, so that a strobe light could be used to check the setting. Access for this was provided by a cover in the primary chaincase.

The electric controls were amended to a toggle light switch in the headlamp shell, still with the ammeter and two warning lights, while the ignition switch was moved to a mounting in the left fork shroud. The forks themselves had modified damping and the front hub was revised to a twin-leading-shoe brake with ventilated backplate. For this one year, the operating cable swept in from the rear to connect to the front cam lever which was linked to the rear one by an adjustable rod. The 1968 finish was in Hi-Fi scarlet and silver in the style used for the decade.

The final year of the 1960s brought more developments to details and another tank badge in the form of a picture frame enclosing the marque name, while the rear units lost their covers in the style of the times. An

Further electrical changes for 1969 were to twin windtone horns with relay and an RM21 alternator with encapsulated stator. On the outside of the engine a balance pipe was fitted between the exhausts close to the ports. The front brake operating linkage was amended so that the cable could run more neatly down the fork leg and thus the lower cam lever became a bell-crank. Models for the USA were fitted with

The conical front hub introduced for 1971 with twin leading shoe brake whose cam levers were too short for full effectiveness.

oil pressure switch appeared in the front of the timing cover and shared the ignition warning light in the headlamp shell. Thus, if it stayed on when the engine was running, it meant that there was no oil pressure and a stop was imperative. There was also a general change over to Unified threads for the screw fastenings, which meant that many parts no longer interchanged with those of the past.

a grab-rail which ran round the back of the seat and bolted to the seat pan itself. The finish changed yet again to Olympic Flame and silver in the earlier style.

The engine breathing system was altered for 1970 with the removal of the timed valve driven by the inlet camshaft. Instead, the crankcase was vented to the chaincase and an outlet stub was bolted to the rear of this, high above the rear sprocket.

A baffle went inside the case to control the gas flow and provide a catchment for oil to feed to the primary chain. On the outside the grab rail was incorporated with the lifting handle and no longer fitted to the seat itself. Otherwise the Bonneville was unaltered but the style of finish was amended. The tank was in Astral red with silver side panels which encompassed both badge and kneegrips, while the mudguards were in the same red with silver stripes. Otherwise it was black and chrome-plating as before.

This brought the unit-construction T120 to a point where it underwent some major changes. Some of the reasons behind these and the great trauma they brought in their wake had their roots back in time but the overall result reflected the errors of a remote design department and poor management.

Thus, for many enthusiasts the Bonneville from the late 1960s became the preferred model to buy and ride.

Oil-in-frame & five gears

By 1970 the T120 had been unchanged in any major way for a good few years and was having to sell against much stiffer opposition. To combat this, an extensive revamp was called for and one result was a good number of parts that became common to Triumph and BSA thanks to group engineering.

Among the common parts were the basic frame, front forks, both hubs, the air cleaner box and a host of detail parts. The results were announced with an extravagant launch for both marques, held in November 1970, when ranges of both new and much revised models were seen. Some were achieved by simple badge engineering for the two makes, but others retained their individual identities.

Behind the lavish front, matters were far from well for the group was in deep financial trouble, compounded by some major technical problems with its 1971 range. As a result, some models were quickly dropped, the company never tooled-

Bonneville T120 for 1972 with modified frame to reduce the excessive seat height of the first oil-bearing design.

up for others and the revised T120 shared problems with the 654 cc BSA twins, which used the same basic frame.

The 1971 Bonneville was built as the T120 for the home market and T120R for export to the USA but the differences were minimal and essentially cosmetic or to suit different legal needs. Both were powered by the familiar engine unit, which was little altered, but the oil pressure valve became a one-piece assembly and it lost its indicator button.

In the gearbox a leaf spring replaced the coil spring for the camplate location, while the twin exhaust pipes ended in megaphone shaped silencers. There were new air filter boxes, one on each side, which each comprised two mould-ings, the whole forming one neat assembly. The outer parts had imitation louvres formed in them which gave them some style.

While the engine unit was familiar, the frame was totally new and carried the engine oil within its massive main tube. This formed both top and seat tube in one with the oil filler cap at the bend, just in front of the dualseat nose. The oil filter went in the bottom of the seat tube and thus became the base of the oil tank, while there were pipes inserted as needed for feed and return plus a rocker box supply.

The remainder of the frame included duplex downtubes which ran back under the engine and then up to the rear unit mountings. A seat loop joined these to the main frame tube and there were suitable cross-

USA form of the 1973 T120R Bonneville with high bars but otherwise much as the home market model.

The 1974 home market Bonneville out on test and delivering in much the same manner as always.

tubes to create the first one-piece, all-welded frame used by the Bonneville. Minor details included lugs on the headstock for a fairing, centre stand, prop stand and good support for the rear fork.

This went back to a form that had the legs extended forward of the cross-piece to carry the bushes but the spindle was now supported by side-plates as well as in the seat tube lug. It was a much better design and the fork continued to be controlled by Girling units minus covers and fitted with 110 lb rate springs.

At the front went slimline forks with internal springs and no gaiters to protect the stanchions. The fork legs were cast aluminium and the wheel spindle caps were retained on four studs for better support. The hydraulic damper in each leg was revised while the head races were changed to taper-roller bearings and the option of a steering damper remained.

Both wheels had new conical hubs cast in light alloy but the rear was no longer quickly detachable. Steel rims continued to be used, the front carrying a 3.25 x 19 in. tyre and the rear a 4.00 x 18 in. one. The brakes were also new and the 8 in. front had twin leading shoes oper-

Twin Concentrics for the 1972 Bonneville mounted to inlet tracts which bolted rather than screwed to the head.

ated by very short cam levers. These levers acted as the inner and outer cable stops and click adjusters at each shoe end enabled them to be set. The backplate was cast with an air-scoop plus exit holes for the air used to cool the drum and shoes. At the rear went a 7 in. single-leading-shoe brake, with a torque arm to anchor the backplate and rod operation from the left-side foot pedal.

The front mudguard was held by a single fore-and-aft stay on each side which was clamped to the fork leg by a bracket mounted in rubber bushes. The rear mudguard kept the combined lifting and grab handle

with this carrying the side reflectors, but the turn indicators were fitted to the rear lamp bracket. The indicators and other electrical functions were controlled by Lucas switches and buttons built into the handlebar control lever blocks but without identifying labels or much in the way of ergonomics. All machines were built with American style high-rise handlebars as standard.

The main light switch remained in the headlamp shell, along with three warning lights but no ammeter. The shell was pan-shaped, and thus much shallower than before, being held by a pair of bent wires which were rubber mounted to the fork crowns. The shell fixings also acted as supports for the front turn signals. The ignition switch was moved to the right-hand side panel, aft of the air cleaner box, and there was a matching panel on the left. The rest of the electrics went under the seat with several items on a single mounting plate.

The model began the year with a 3 gallon petrol tank but some months later a somewhat slab-sided one, holding 4 gallons, appeared for the home market. The finish in both cases was in Tiger gold and black, the same colours being used for the mudguards. The rest of the machine was as before with the painted items in black and the headlamp shell chrome-plated. Instrumentation continued to be speedometer and rev-counter but these were mounted in rubber cups in brackets fixed to the fork top nuts.

All this was fine as far as the machine went, but then the problems began to appear. The poor decisions, the separation of design effort and inadequate planning struck home for the tooling, essential jigs and fixtures were not ready on time. For a while the factory kept going by building the smaller, largely unchanged, Tiger 100 model, but soon came to a standstill.

Feverish work, always expensive and prone to errors, brought the production line to something near a

Final T120 year was really 1974 but some of these machines did not emerge until 1975 due to the Meriden sit-in.

state of readiness but then a further blow fell. The engine unit could not be fitted into the frame. Removal of the rocker boxes was found to overcome this problem but introduced another in that the boxes could not be re-installed.

Eventually, the engine's detail parts were modified enough for assembly to commence at the end of 1970, really far too late commercially to meet all the needs of the vital American market. It was then realised that the seat height was excessive, and equally so on the BSA twins, mostly because the designers at Umberslade Hall, the group design centre for BSA and Triumph, had little motorcycle knowledge and

no real contact with the experts at either Meriden or Small Heath. The design centre was closed at the start of 1972 but, by then, the damage had been done.

Other factors were involved, but the whole group was now in serious trouble, so measures for 1972 were at panic level. Most alterations to the Bonneville were made to reduce the seat height, which was done with a revised frame and new dualseat. There were a host of detail changes involved with this but, despite the problems, there were other, major alterations.

One change affected the cylinder head and rocker boxes and came in during the year. The head was al-

John Holder who shared the winning pre-unit Bonneville at the 1961 Thruxton 500 mile race.

The Triumph engine was always popular for sprints and this one has a Shorrock blower to help as well as enlarged capacity.

tered to take exhaust pipes that simply pushed into the ports, rather than over stubs, so the finned clamps became purely cosmetic. On the inlet side the screw-in tracts were replaced by adaptors that fitted on the mounting studs of the carburettors to space them away from the head. The rocker boxes were altered so that a single flat cover on each replaced the two access caps of old. The box was machined to suit and had four screws to hold the cover, which gave much better access to the rockers.

To keep up with the times a five-speed gearbox became available and models with this fitted were listed as the T120V or T120RV. The new box went into the existing crank-case but, as well as the gears and shafts, there was a new camplate, quadrant, three selector forks and sleeve gear bearing. The sleeve gear itself was fitted with needle races for the mainshaft. The finish was much as in 1971 but in Tiger gold and Cold white.

For 1973, the T120 was joined by the larger T140 (covered by another book in this series), which was to take the Triumph name through most of the 1980s. With it came changes that were adopted by the T120 and included a triplex primary chain and suitable sprockets.

Most of the obvious changes were to the front end where a 10 in. disc brake with hydraulic operation was fitted. This meant a new hub which was made in two halves. These were held together by the same four bolts that held the disc in place. The hub was spoked into the same rim, fitted with the same tyre as before while the rear wheel was unaltered.

The forks, yokes and front mudguard were changed with the reappearance of gaiters and top shrouds. Each of the latter was in ing lights.

The wire stay fixing of the front mudguard was replaced by the older style with front and rear loops plus a central bridge. At the rear of the machine the Girling units were shorter to help reduce the seat height and the silencers became longer and slimmer, with curved and tapered end cones. The outer air-

Peter Butler rode production Triumphs very successfully for a number of years and is here seen at Brands Hatch in 1968.

three parts, with a headlamp bracket fixed to the shroud round the fork leg, with a rubber block between them to reduce the effects of vibration. Once again, the left bracket carried the ignition switch, while the headlamp shell reverted to its earlier, deeper style, carrying a toggle light switch and three warn-box mouldings lost their louvres.

Both four- and five-speed models were built and minor changes continued to occur during the year. One was a new form of rev-counter-drive gearbox and another affected the rocker box covers. These gained extra fixings at each end to make six in all, which meant a change to the boxes. In the gearbox there was a return to an index plunger for the camplate as of old.

The finish was now in Hi-Fi vermilion with gold side panels for the tank which continued to hold 4 gallons for the home market. In the USA a slim 2 gallon tank, in the same colours, was fitted and all versions had chrome-plated mudguards. The USA version also lacked the fork gaiters, had raised bars and its own specification silencers.

Meanwhile, the group itself had gone from bad to worse with involvement of the City and the government. From this came Norton Villiers Triumph, or NVT, and numerous plans for salvaging what was left of the industry, of which BSA itself had gone, but Triumph and Norton remained.

In September 1973, a meeting was to be held at Meriden, but before it took place the workforce learned, from local papers, that their plant was to close. This, they refused to accept, so that night the factory was taken over and the famous Meriden sit-in began. It was to last 18 months, but early in 1974 there was a general election and a change to a Labour government. Left-winger Tony Benn became involved, keen to promote his ideals of the workers' co-operative but, although eventually this was set up, it was to have a difficult life.

During this period the Bonneville was built to a 1974 specification with no steering damper option and tank colours of purple and Cold white. A number of machines were produced late in 1973, but the sit-in blockade stopped further production until mid-1974. More emerged for a period up to late 1974, when the blockade was fully imposed once more, after which it was March 1975 before the machines appeared again.

Those produced then were the final T120 models, and still to the 1974 specification, to clear the decks for the future. From the middle of the year, only T140 machines with a left-side gearchange, to suit USA legislation, were built - as 1976 models. Thus, the T120 Bonneville reached its end in its 1974 form, despite the final machines having been completed in the following year.

It was a sad and messy end for such a successful motorcycle but the name, the style and the legend were to continue with the T140 into the late 1980s. With the classic revival of that decade the T120 became, once more, one of the cult machines.

Competition T120

The 649 cc Bonneville had a tremendous record in production racing during the 1960s when it became THE machine to run and to beat. There were victories in the important Thruxton 500 miles and Production TT events that were recorded and advertised but along with these came hundreds of wins in lesser events.

At club level, Bonnevilles raced in all manners of condition, some coming straight from the street; their riders egged on by their mates. Often, such entries had a machine with an exaggerated riding position, but most soon learned from the fast men and some would do very well in time.

Many well-known names rode the T120, John Hartle being the winner of the first Production TT in 1967

Bill Johnson stands beside his streamlined record breaker on Bonneville flats, the location the T120 was aptly named after.

The twin engined Gyronaut X-1 ridden by Bob Leppan on show in London.

and Malcolm Uphill taking the honours in 1969, when he became the first to lap the circuit at over 100 mph on a production machine. At Thruxton and Brands Hatch the model was successful in the 500 mile races in 1961, 1966, 1967 and 1969 with a variety of riders including Roy Pickrell, factory tester Percy Tait and multiple world champion Phil Read.

The Bonneville engine was used for sprints by many, many riders and for world record attempts. The latter followed the success of Johnny Allen, who had run his T110-powered streamliner at 214 mph in 1956,

a record never sanctioned by the FIM. In 1962, Bill Johnson ran his machine at 224 mph, which was accepted as the official record and, in 1966, Bob Leppan used two 649 cc engines to run at 245 mph. Again, this was not recognised, but the Americans had long ceased to worry about the FIM and its odd ways. The machine used was a full streamliner called Gyronaut X-1 and its engines ran on alcohol fuel.

All the records were created at Bonneville salt flats in Utah from where the T120 took its name - a nice touch for one of the great motorcycles of all time.

Bonneville Specifications

All models have two cylinders, overhead valves and twin carburettors

Model	T120	T120	T120	T120R	T120R	T120R
years	1959-62	1963-70	1971	1960-62	1963-70	1971-73
bore mm	71	71	71	71	71	71
stroke mm	82	82	82	82	82	82
capacity cc	649	649	649	649	649	649
comp. ratio	8.5	8.5[1]	9.0	8.5	8.5[1]	9.0
carb type	376	376[2]	930	376	376[2]	930
carb size	1-1/16	1-1/16[3]	30 mm	1-1/16	1-1/16[4]	30 mm
ignition	mag	coil	coil	mag	coil	coil
electrics volts	6	6[5]	12	6	6[5]	12
no.gears	4	4	4	4	4	4
top gear	4.58[6]	4.84	4.95	4.67[7]	4.84	4.95
petrol - gall	4[8]	3 or 4[9]	3 or 4	3[10]	3 or 4[11]	2.4 or 4[12]
front tyre	3.25x19	3.25x18[13]	3.25x19	3.25x19	3.25x18[13]	3.25x19
rear tyre	3.50x19[14]	3.50x18	4.00x18	3.50x19[14]	4.00x18	4.00x18
front brake dia	8	8	8	8	8	8[15]
rear brake dia	7	7	7	7	7	7
wheelbase in.	55.7[16]	55	56	55.7[16]	55	56

[1] - 1967-9.0
[2] - 1964-389, 1968-930
[3] - 1964-1-1/16, 1968-9 30mm
[4] - 1964-1-1/18, 1966-1-3/16,1968-30 mm
[5] - 1966-12
[6] - 1960-4.67, 1961-4.89
[7] - 1961-4.89
[8] - 1961-3, 1962-3 or 4
[9] - 1968-4
[10] - 1962-4
[11] - 1964-3, 1966-2
[12] - 1973-2
[13] - 1967-3.25x19
[14] - 1961-4.00x18
[15] - 1973-10 disc
[16] - 1961-56.5

Bonneville Specifications

Model	T120RV	T120V	T120C	T120C	T120TT
years	1972-74	1974	1960-62	1963-65	1964-67
bore mm	71	71	71	71	71
stroke mm	82	82	82	82	82
capacity cc	649	649	649	649	649
comp. ratio	9.0	9.0	8.5	8.5	11.0
carb type	930	930	376	389	389
carb size	30 mm	30 mm	1-1/16	1-1/8	1-3/16
ignition	coil	coil	mag	coil	ET
electrics volts	12	12	6	6	-
no.gears	5	5	4	4	4
top gear	4.95	4.95	4.67[1]	5.11	5.41
petrol - gall	2.4 or 4[2]	4	3	3 or 4[3]	3[4]
front tyre	3.25x19	3.25x19	3.25x19	3.25x19	3.50x19
rear tyre	4.00x18	4.00x18	4.00x18	4.00x18	4.00x18
front brake dia	8[5]	10 disc	8	8	8
rear brake dia	7	7	7	7	7
wheelbase in.	56	56	55.7[6]	55	55

[1] - 1961-4.89
[2] - 1973-2 or 4
[3] - 1964-3
[4] - 1966-2
[5] - 1973-10 disc
[6] - 1961-56.5